CAMBRIDGE LIBRARY COLLECTION

Books of enduring scholarly value

History

The books reissued in this series include accounts of historical events and movements by eye-witnesses and contemporaries, as well as landmark studies that assembled significant source materials or developed new historiographical methods. The series includes work in social, political and military history on a wide range of periods and regions, giving modern scholars ready access to influential publications of the past.

The Manuscripts in the Library at Lambeth Palace

M. R. James (1862-1936) is probably best remembered as a writer of chilling ghost stories, but he was an outstanding scholar of medieval literature and palaeography, who served both as Provost of King's College, Cambridge, and as Director of the Fitzwilliam Museum, and many of his stories reflect his academic background. His detailed descriptive catalogues of manuscripts owned by colleges, cathedrals and museums are still of value to scholars today. This book, first published in 1900, lists about six hundred medieval manuscripts in the library at Lambeth Palace, most of them collected by Archbishop Bancroft (d. 1610). These were sent to Cambridge University Library during Cromwell's Protectorate, and returned to Lambeth Palace at the Restoration. Referring to several early inventories, James succeeds in tracing the ownership of many of the manuscripts back to English monastic houses dissolved at the Reformation including Durham Priory, Lanthony (near Gloucester), and Ely.

Cambridge University Press has long been a pioneer in the reissuing of out-of-print titles from its own backlist, producing digital reprints of books that are still sought after by scholars and students but could not be reprinted economically using traditional technology. The Cambridge Library Collection extends this activity to a wider range of books which are still of importance to researchers and professionals, either for the source material they contain, or as landmarks in the history of their academic discipline.

Drawing from the world-renowned collections in the Cambridge University Library, and guided by the advice of experts in each subject area, Cambridge University Press is using state-of-the-art scanning machines in its own Printing House to capture the content of each book selected for inclusion. The files are processed to give a consistently clear, crisp image, and the books finished to the high quality standard for which the Press is recognised around the world. The latest print-on-demand technology ensures that the books will remain available indefinitely, and that orders for single or multiple copies can quickly be supplied.

The Cambridge Library Collection will bring back to life books of enduring scholarly value (including out-of-copyright works originally issued by other publishers) across a wide range of disciplines in the humanities and social sciences and in science and technology.

The Manuscripts in the Library at Lambeth Palace

MONTAGUE RHODES JAMES

CAMBRIDGE
UNIVERSITY PRESS

CAMBRIDGE UNIVERSITY PRESS

Cambridge, New York, Melbourne, Madrid, Cape Town, Singapore,
São Paolo, Delhi, Dubai, Tokyo

Published in the United States of America by Cambridge University Press, New York

www.cambridge.org
Information on this title: www.cambridge.org/9781108011327

This edition first published 1900
This digitally printed version 2010

ISBN 978-1-108-01132-7 Paperback

THE MANUSCRIPTS

IN THE

LIBRARY AT LAMBETH PALACE

PUBLICATIONS : OCTAVO SERIES

No. XXXIII

THE MANUSCRIPTS

IN THE

LIBRARY AT LAMBETH PALACE

BY

MONTAGUE RHODES JAMES, Litt.D.

FELLOW AND TUTOR OF KING'S COLLEGE,
DIRECTOR OF THE FITZWILLIAM MUSEUM.

Cambridge:
PRINTED FOR THE CAMBRIDGE ANTIQUARIAN SOCIETY.

THE MANUSCRIPTS IN THE LIBRARY AT LAMBETH PALACE.

In Wood's *Athenae Oxonienses* (ii. 519) there is a short biography of John Theyer. He was born apparently in 1597 and his career—not an eventful one—does not now concern me particularly. It is the conclusion of Wood's article which supplies me with a text: "His death hapned at *Cowper's-hill* [near Gloucester] on the 25th of *Aug.* in sixteen hundred seventy and three, and two days after <he> was buried among his Ancestors in the Church-yard at *Brockworth*, particularly near to the grave of his grandfather — *Theyer*, who had married the sister of one *Hart* the last Prior of *Langthony* near *Glocester*. He then left behind him a Library of ancient Manuscripts consisting of the number of about 800, which he himself had for the most part collected. The Foundation of it was laid by his grandfather, who had them from Prior *Hart*, and he from the Library of *Langthony* when it was dissolved, besides Household stuff belonging to that Priory. Afterwards *Charles Theyer* (grandson to our author *John Theyer*, who in his last will had bequeathed them to him) did offer to sell them to the University of *Oxon*, but the price being too great, they were sold to *Robert Scot*, of *London*, bookseller, who soon after sold them to his Majesty, King *Ch. II.*, to be reposed in his Library at S. *James's*, he having first, as I have been informed, cull'd them."

Following up the *data* of this paragraph, we are led in the first place to ask whether any record exists of the contents of the Theyer Collection before its absorption into the Royal Library. We find that in Bernard's *Catalogi Manuscriptorum Angliae* (1697), ii. pp. 198—203, is a list of 312 MSS. belonging to Charles Theyer, of Gloucestershire : and a comparison of this list with Casley's Catalogue of the Royal MSS. shews that with very few exceptions the books enumerated now form part of the Royal Library. In other words, the collection of Charles Theyer, described by Bernard, is that which Charles II. bought. It is clear that when Bernard's Catalogue was issued the Theyer MSS. must have been for some years at St James's: but I do not find any note of the fact either in Preface or Appendix. It will be further noticed that the number of books (312) differs widely from that specified by Wood (about 800). An explanation of this fact is not immediately forthcoming.

We should expect at this stage of our investigation to find that the Theyer MSS. in the Royal Library were traceable in large part to Lanthony Priory. That, however, is not the case. Of a large number which I have myself examined, not more than two or three are Lanthony books. Worcester and Gloucester have contributed largely to the collection : and this is not surprising when we know that the ancestral abode of the Theyers was in the immediate neighbourhood of Gloucester. But as to Lanthony—clearly there is something more than meets the eye in the history as given by Wood. We can hardly doubt that he is correct in his account of the connexion between the old Theyer and Prior Hart, and the presence of many books from Lanthony on Theyer's shelves. We also see that these books must have been diverted to some other quarter before the purchase of the collection by Charles II. Can we at this time of day ascertain either when the diversion took place, or where the Lanthony books are now ? I believe we can.

It would clearly be a very great help if we could arm ourselves with a document showing what books were in the Library whose relics we are pursuing. Such a document is very fortunately accessible. The Harleian MS. 460 contains a catalogue of the Lanthony Library made in 1380, which has been printed by M. H. Omont of the *Bibliothèque Nationale*[1]. It enumerates some 500 volumes, and at a later stage a word will be said as to its arrangement and contents.

With this catalogue before us we are in a better position to prosecute our researches. Yet I doubt if anything but an accident could conduct us to a successful issue. And such an accident has befallen me. In January, 1899, I was permitted by the kindness of His Grace the Archbishop of Canterbury, seconded by the prompt assistance of Mr Kershaw, the Librarian of Lambeth Palace, to make a systematic examination of the MSS. in the Archiepiscopal Library. It was my hope that among them there would prove to be a large contingent from Canterbury: but the Canterbury books, though interesting, are not numerous. To some extent, however, I was compensated for this disappointment by the discovery that a very large number of the Lambeth MSS. are from Lanthony Priory.

I have mentioned the name of this establishment a good many times without any explanatory note. So I will just remark here that there are three Lanthonies known to fame. The first 'Lanthonia prima' was an Augustinian Priory in Wales, founded in 1108; the second, 'Lanthonia secunda,' a daughter of the first, and by far the more important, founded in 1136 in the outskirts of Gloucester; the third, Lanthony of the present day, an establishment presided over by the Rev. Mr Lyne, purports to have some connexion with the order of St Benedict. Throughout this paper when reference is made simply to Lanthony, the second Lanthony—that at Gloucester— is intended. It is of this house that we possess the Library catalogue; and perhaps it will be well to place here the few words which have to be said about that.

The books are entered in order as they stood on the shelves. There were five cupboards (*armarii*), containing respectively five, four, five, six, and one, shelves. It is natural to suppose

---

[1] In *Centralblatt für Bibliotheks-Wissenschaft*, 1892, 207—222.

that the fifth press, to which the one shelf belongs, was intended to provide for further acquisitions[1].

The other characteristic of the catalogue is that it is digested into subjects.

The first bookcase contained mainly Bibles, and glosses and commentaries upon various books of the Bible. In the second were the writings of Clement of Lanthony, the most prominent scholar the house produced, and those of Jerome, Ambrose, Gregory, Bede, Isidore, and others. The third began with Augustine, and contained also Hugo of St Victor, and minor theologians, while on its fifth shelf were the books on physic. The fourth was the most varied in contents, comprising Canon Law, Miscellaneous Divinity, History, Grammar, Poetry, Philosophy, and Custumaries[2]. The fifth had dictionaries and a few service-books, together with some miscellaneous volumes of the theological class.

Whether considered in the light of its catalogue, or in that of the extant volumes, this collection as a whole does not rise above mediocrity. The house produced, as I have said, but one writer who attained anything like celebrity, in its Prior Clement. His Harmony of the Gospels is a sufficiently common book. Nine or ten volumes are specially connected with his name in the catalogue. One among these I have identified, and believe to be in his autograph. It is a commentary on the Acts, and is among the few Lanthony books

---

[1] The number of volumes in the several shelves varies very curiously. The annexed table in which Roman numerals are used to designate the cupboards, and Arabic for the shelves, will shew this :

I 1	10 vols.	II 1	8 vols.	III 1	12 vols.	IV 1	20 vols.	V 1	21 vols.
2	13 ,,	2	14 ,,	2	20 ,,	2	24 ,,		
3	24 ,,	3	16 ,,	3	18 ,,	3	35 ,,		
4	13 ,,	4	20 ,,	4	17 ,,	4	64 ,,		
5	40 ,,			5	21 ,,	5	32 ,,		
						6	41 ,,		

[2] Namely, the Custumaries of St Victor's, Cluny, the Chartreuse, Merton, and an old one of Lanthony itself,

in the British Museum (Royal 2.D.V). Otherwise, the catalogue contains very few entries that excite curiosity. The MSS. themselves are for the most part good normal twelfth century books. There is seldom anything earlier. A Psalter with English glosses (no. 427) is almost the only one I can point to which is older than the monastery itself.

As I have said, the number of Lambeth MSS. which ·I assign to Lanthony is very large—well over a hundred. The question will inevitably occur to my readers—on what grounds is each individual book identified ? In a large number of cases we have the definite inscription, *liber Lanthonie* or the like to guide us. Where this is absent I have very often been led to the mark by the occurrence of a certain handwriting on the fly-leaves. It is a hand of the xvth century, which has furnished a great many of the books with tables of contents. Sometimes I have found it coupled with a Lanthony inscription, sometimes alone. In either case the provenance is certain. Then there is the name of a certain Canon Morgan, of Carmarthen, who may possibly be the writer of the tables of contents aforesaid : this, again, may occur either in conjunction with the other indications, or apart from them. Lastly, there are cases in which the contents of a volume, and its presence side by side with a number of books which are certainly from Lanthony, enable me with fair certainty to identify it with some entry in the catalogue. Doubtful items of course there are in my list : but I think it will be found that the evidence is fairly given in most instances.

I will now treat shortly of the Lambeth MSS. as a collection, and try to bring out the chief points of interest in their history. The manuscript library at Lambeth consists of somewhat over 1200 volumes, which are divided into several distinct collections. First, there are the *Codices Lambethani*, numbering nearly 600, collected mostly by Archbishop Bancroft (d. 1610). Then come Wharton's papers, the collections of Sir George Carew (chiefly Irish), of Archbishop Tenison, of Bishop Gibson : next the *Miscellanei*, and last the MSS. of Archbishop Manners-Sutton. It is only with the first block, the *Codices Lambethani*, that I am concerned now. The later collections are for the most part papers, of great interest, but of rather recent date.

It is well known that during the Protectorate the Lambeth books were made over to the University of Cambridge, and remained there until the Restoration. In Mr Bradshaw's *Collected Papers* a detailed account of the transaction may be readily found. Among the MSS. in the University Library there still remain several catalogues of the printed books and MSS. received by the University from Lambeth: and a very slight inspection of these serves to show that the Lanthony books already formed part of the Archbishop's Library. Of the book-buying archbishops before the Civil War we know that it was Bancroft who was the principal contributor to the Lambeth Library. His successor, Abbot, though he did add to the collection, did not, so far as I can discover, achieve much in the way of acquiring MSS. We must suppose provisionally, I think, assuming that Wood's story of Prior Hart of Lanthony is true, that Archbishop Bancroft bought from the elder Theyer a large number of MSS. including the greater part of the books which had belonged to Prior Hart; and we must suppose that Wood was mistaken in thinking that the Theyer MSS. passed intact into the possession of John and of Charles Theyer.

That is the last, I think, which need be said about Lanthony for some time. The most interesting of the Lambeth MSS. come from other sources, at which we will glance briefly.

Canterbury naturally claims the first place in our list: its contribution is interesting if not large. The Gospel-book of MacDurnan, that famous specimen of Irish art, was given to Christ Church by King Æthelstan. How it came to Lambeth is not known: but it has a binding on it, and red chalk marks therein, which shew beyond question that it was once the property of Archbishop Parker. Sixteen other Lambeth MSS. are from Christ Church. Taking them roughly in order as they stand on the shelves, we note a late but very important obituary, of which Wharton made large use in his *Anglia Sacra*: an early copy of Anselm's Letters; a volume of Richard,

Abbot of Préaux, upon Genesis, whereof the second volume is
at Trinity College, Cambridge ; the Canterbury Letters, edited
in the Rolls Series by the Bishop of Oxford ; and a fine Psalter
which belonged to John Holyngborne. He was a monk of the
Priory late in the xvth century, and seems to have been active
either in collecting old books, or at least in writing his name in
books which already belonged to his monastery. I have
met his name rather frequently. The well-known pictured
Apocalypse of the xiiith century (no. 209) is regarded by the
authorities of the Palæographical Society as being a production
of Canterbury artists. It contains the arms and effigy of a
Lady de Quincey.

From St Augustine's Abbey we have eleven volumes. The
oldest—of the eighth or ninth century—contains our only copy
of a short tract by Victorinus, *De fabrica mundi*. In another
are some palimpsest leaves of an early Kalendar. A third is a
chronicle which is attributed in the Abbey Catalogue to Sprot
or Sport.

Bury St Edmund's has six volumes to its credit. Five of
them were unknown to me when I wrote my Essay on its
Library : which Essay begins, I am glad to say, to need a
supplement. The additions here are of considerable interest.
A copy of the Arithmetic and Music of Boethius was once the
property of Dr John Dee. I dare not now embark upon a
disquisition I should much enjoy concerning that unlucky
scholar's MSS., the sources whence he obtained them, and their
present resting places. Many years ago Mr J. O. Halliwell
printed the list of his MSS. for the Camden Society ; and of late
it has become possible for me to detect and locate a very fair
number of his most interesting possessions in this department.
He drew largely, I may say, from St Augustine's, Canterbury,
through the medium, I suspect, of John Twine ; and a great
many of his books are, with Brian Twyne's library, now at
Corpus Christi College, Oxford.

There is further an early MS. of Alcuin's Letters from Bury,
at Lambeth, as early, perhaps, as any that exists. It is bound
up with the *Collations* of Cassianus, and has been so bound since

the early part of the fifteenth century at least. There is a title-page in the volume describing both books, and this description is couched in words which recur in the *Catalogus scriptorum* of John Boston, of Bury. Moreover, it is in the handwriting which I have always suspected to be the autograph of that remarkable bibliographer. Lastly, I will mention a Bible, rather a good one, of the ordinary thirteenth century type, but made interesting by a long note in sixteenth century English. In this the pedigree of the book is traced from the year 1384 to a date very near that of its absorption into the Lambeth Library.

Durham Priory sends a small but very noteworthy set of books. This foundation has certainly preserved more of its original library *in situ* than any other in the country: but still the number of Durham MSS. which I have encountered in various English libraries is growing to a remarkable figure. The items at Lambeth include first a sumptuous copy of the *Historia Aurea* of John of Tynemouth, and second a tenth century copy of Ennodius in Carolingian minuscules, which once belonged to John Foxe, the martyrologist.

If adequate materials for the investigation could be found, the question of the history and contents of the Library of Ely Priory would be a very appropriate and interesting subject for some members of this society to take up. As yet, I have hit upon no trace of a catalogue, nor seen any document which gives the least idea of the importance or extent of the collection. Two clues there are to the identification of Ely books, which I believe to be unfailing. One is the presence in the margin of this sign $\overset{+}{\text{II}}$; the other, the occurrence of the name of Robert Stewarde, which is usually accompanied by a sketch of the Stuart arms. This Robert was the last Prior of Ely, and was fond of writing his name in books. So was Augustine Styward, a relation of Robert's, who was Mayor of Norwich. I have set down seven Lambeth books as possibly from Ely: but in the case of some I waver between Ely and Norwich.

One of the better known Lambeth MSS. is a volume which contains three distinct parts. First a late xvth century paper

copy of Roger Bacon's *Opus Tertium*—very likely from Oxford
—used by Mr J. S. Brewer. Next, a tenth century Aldhelm
with one fine Saxon drawing, reproduced as the frontispiece to
Todd's *Catalogue*; and last, a MS. from Lanthony. It is satis-
factory to me to be able to point out the provenance of the
Aldhelm. On its fly-leaf is the inscription "cxxx. al. ca."
Marks like this, consisting of a Roman number, followed by
the abbrevations "al. ca." or "al. p.," always mean that the book
containing them was once the property of the Abbey of the
Holy Cross at Waltham. Another book in this same collection
gives proof of this assertion (though the fact is known and has
been noted by Macray in his *Annals of the Bodleian*). It is
marked "cxli. al. ca.,' and has, besides, a distich beginning

Crux sibi sancta librum de Waltham vendicat istum.

The meaning of the letters "al. ca." and "al. p.," as yet un-
interpreted, I take to be "almariolum canonicorum" and
"almariolum prioris."

There is another highly interesting composite volume
(no. 149), of which the second part comes, I believe, from
Lanthony, but the first, a tenth century Bede on the Apocalypse, certainly does not. It has at the end an inscription in
fine large capitals (printed by Todd) to the effect that in the
year 1018 it was given by the Alderman Æthelward to a Church
of St Mary, at a place whose name has been entirely obliterated,
partly at least by the use of galls. On the same page and not
noted by Todd is another short inscription in green capitals,
"In nomine Domini. Amen. Leofricus pater."

Now in 1018 the see of Devon was still at Crediton, and
Leofric, a great book-man, as we know, was its bishop: and its
church was dedicated to St Mary: and an *Expositio Bede
super Apocalypsim* is in the list of the Latin books which
Leofric procured for Exeter. Crediton therefore must be the
name that stood in the erasure. Leofric may have scratched it
out when he transferred the book to Exeter, and a later attempt
to revive it has completed its deletion.

For Exeter MSS. in bulk we have to go to the Bodleian,
where, owing to the surprising liberality of an early Chapter,

there are over eighty. In them we very soon learn to recognise a hand that writes descriptive titles and the like. It is that of John Grandison, Bishop of Exeter (1327—1369), and no mean scholar, but less known now-a-days for that than for the screen crowded with imagery wherewith he masked the western front of his Cathedral Church. There are traces of his literary activity at Lambeth. In a twelfth century Augustine he writes that he gives it to his Church of Exeter, because he had taken great pains with the correction of it at Paris : and elsewhere in the book is a note written by him when studying at that famous university (in 1314).

Such are some of the more immediately interesting results of my examination of the external history of the Lambeth MSS. Naturally many riddles remain unsolved. I shall hope to learn in the future what library was the home of no. 52, marked " de sexto ordine xlii^{us}." I suspect it of having come from one of the great London houses. I should be glad also to throw some light on the great Bible (no. 3, 4) of which a description and some illustrations will be found in Mr Kershaw's interesting volume on the *Art Treasures of the Lambeth Library.* That the two volumes (which were not originally connected) are of English and not German execution I am well convinced. The beautiful Psalter (no. 233) I believe to be East Anglian ; but a study of its heraldry is needed before a verdict can be pronounced. It intimately resembles in certain particulars a MS. acquired not long ago by the Fitzwilliam Museum from the late Mr William Morris.

It seems not inappropriate, in conclusion, to reckon up shortly the services which the occupants of the see of Canterbury have rendered to the world in the preservation of ancient literature. Whether we have any books which St Augustine may confidently be said to have handled is doubtful. Theodore of Tarsus has been persistently credited with the importation of several extant MSS., but one only—the Laudian MS. of the Acts—can be now said even to have been possibly his, or connected with him. From Plegmund (891) we have the blackened fragments of a copy of Gregory's *Pastoral Care* (Cotton, Tiberius B. xi.). Dunstan, as archbishop, owned no single book that we have now. The one that has the best claim to have been his dates from the time when he was Abbot of Glastonbury. In the Christ Church Catalogue Lanfranc is credited with a Homiliary, a Priscian, and three copies of Paul's Epistles. These I have never seen: but at Trinity College, Cambridge, there is a *Corpus Canonum* which he brought to England from Bec, and many relics exist, both there and elsewhere, of the school of calligraphy which I believe him to have introduced. To Anselm, perhaps the greatest writer of them all, I can unfortunately assign not one book; but St Thomas à Becket collected a large and valuable library in whose composition I seem to trace the influence of his friend, John of Salisbury. At present I have marked about half-a-dozen extant books as having been his property. Stephen Langton gave six volumes to Christ Church: one remains. Robert Winchelsey about 45: I have identified two. Of the libraries of Mepham, Whittlesea, Courtenay, Chicheley, there are in like manner, inconsiderable remnants. Warham's books are at New College; Cranmer's in many places; Pole's at New College; Parker's at Corpus Christi, Cambridge; Whitgift's (with over 200 MSS.) at Trinity, Cambridge; Bancroft's at Lambeth; Laud's—most numerous of all—in the Bodleian, and at St John's, Oxford. A few waifs have made their way to other places. Juxon and Sheldon were no great collectors: the latter is responsible for a few MSS. at Lambeth. Sancroft's mostly went to Emmanuel College: others are among the Tanner MSS. at the Bodleian. Tenison had a large library: part of his MSS. are at Lambeth, and others which were in the Parish Library of St Martin's in the Fields were dispersed in 1861. The best of these are in the British Museum. Wake's are at Christ Church, Oxford. Secker's—mostly autograph Biblical collections—at Lambeth. There also are the Greek MSS. procured for Manners-Sutton.

The list is an impressive one. In this regard, as in many others, I would say with all due respect that the see of Augustine has a lasting claim on the gratitude of England.

CODICES LAMBETHANI.

1. Service book with music   xiv

2. Hugh Broughton's Tables of the
   Prophecies etc. with diagrams   xvi

3, 4. Bible   xii

     3 contains Genesis—4 Regum, Isaias—Malachias, Job, with
pictures, resembling on the whole the great Winchester Bible :
it is of English, not German execution.   alii celo *or* tile terre

     4 contains Psalter—Apocalypse.   sue diuitiis *or* con-
                                         uertendo

     It has no large pictures.
     At the end an erased inscription.
     Kershaw, p. 69.

5. Concordance, etc.   xv   Peterborough

     Has a note on the 'erection' of Peterborough into a Cathe-
dral Church (1541), and the entry ' Thys bowke belongs to the
Library of Peterborow 1541.'   et impinguati

6. St Alban's Chronicle with pictures   xv
     Kershaw, p. 59.

7. Gradual   xv
     Kershaw, p. 40.

8. Radulphus de Diceto etc.   xii, xiii   Lond. St Paul's
     Liber ecclesie Scī Pauli Londoñ.   nomina regionum

     In the Catalogue of 1458 (Dugdale, *History of St Paul's*,
p. 392) under the letter F is entered

     Cronica Radulphi de Diceto.   2 fo. Nomina regionum

9. Lyra super Psalmos etc.—Apoca-
   lypsim   xiv   futuro super
10, 11, 12. Historia aurea Joh. de
   Tynemouth   xiv   Durham
   10. Title: Prima pars Historie auree.
   11. Secunda pars Historie auree cum tabula.
   12. Ff. Tercia pars Historie auree (erasure): a xvth cent.
   prophecy of St Thomas, at end, is signed Ffyshborne.
   In *Catalogi Veteres* (Surtees Society) p. 56 is the entry
   D. Prima pars Historiae Aureae. 2 fo. Baptisimus mortem.
   E. Secunda Pars Historiae Aureae. 2 fo. Franci a Fran-
      cone.
   F. Tertia pars Hist. Aur. cum vitis SS. Etheldredae Sex-
   burgae et Withburgae et cum vitis SS. David Patricii et Bre-
   gurici in principio. 2 fo. quintini martiris corpus.

13. Joh. Andreae super Sextum etc.   xiv   Lanthony
    Given by John Leche.

14. Digest.   xiv   utilitatibus
    The names of Johannes de Newynton and others occur.
    Also: liber Philippi Goter.

15. Printed (N. T. of 'Mazarine' Bible).
    Kershaw, p. 34.

16. Azo super Codicem   xiii   Yorkshire
    Liber Hugonis de Skefding impignoratus Mag. Stephano
    de Hedon pro xl^s (dated 1273).
    Skeffling and Hedon are both in Holderness.

17 wanting

18. Sext, etc.   xiii   Lanthony
    The name (xv) Madoc ap Rys, occurs at the end of art. 2.
                                                 indulgencias

19. Paper, xvi

20. Martyrology etc.   xvi   Chr. Ch. Cant.
    Used by Wharton and others.

21. Innocentius iv super Decretales   xiv   Lanthony
     Given by John Leche : has good Italian ornament.

22. Scala mundi etc.   late xv   anno primo
                                                   or centesimo
     Belonged to Lord Lumley.

23. Alex. Neckam super Cantica etc.   xiv   ? Lanthony
     Has the xvth cent. title and :   ortus *or* quibus
     I^{us} 5^{ti} M.   Perhaps no. 472 in Catalogue.
     On f. 1: Alex. nequam super cantica cum aliis ex dono
     G. Houeden.
     Good borders and initials.

24. (1)   Martinus Polonus   xiv   sanguine
     (2)   Dictionarium Theologicum :
           five columns to a page   xiii   quam esca
     (3)   Document of Abp Warham   xvi

25. Wycliffite Bible.

26. Decretals mut. init.   xv   ei idcirco

27. (1)   Codex Justiniani   xiv   dī ceterarum
     (2)   Comment.   xiii   huiusmodi

28. Unum ex quatuor   xii   Lanthony
     Catalogue no. 11. Zacharias de concordia iiii^{or} Euuangelist-
     arum in uno volumine magno.   (*in libro*) aliter iuuencus
                                            or eodem.   Et cum

29. Cassiodorius in Ps. ci–cl   xiii   Lanthony
     Catalogue 58—60. Cassiod. super Psalt. in tribus voll.
     magnis.

30. Decretals : xvth cent. title   xiii   ? Lanthony
     At the end: liber Radulfi tuprest de Westm̄ precio duarum
     marcarum.   quem abbas

31. Decretals   xiv   astruendam

32. Bradwardine de Causa dei   xiv   quem et *or* cel^{us}
                                                      princeps

33. Ryngsted super Proverbia. London, Franciscans   xv   per tas
 (1) ffrater Tho. Kingston.   (2)   Thome Vmfry sacerdotis
ecclesie S. Pauli.   (3)   Lord Lumley.

34. Wycliffite.   Kershaw, p. 35.

35. Paper.

36. Alexandri Distinctio etc.   xiii   Lanthony
 xvth cent. title headed, In hoc uolumine continentur, etc.
in the Lanthony hand.   tatis exequitur

37. Digest.   xiii   Lanthony
 Legauit mag. Johannes de Leech'. ecclesie Lanthonie iuxta
Gloucestriam.

38. Ps. Chrysostomi opus imperfectum   xv
 In two hands, one like that of Thorney *Miracula B. V. M.*
at Sidney Sussex College.

39. Leges Longobardorum etc.   xiv   Lanthony
 Bequeathed by John Leche : older inscription liber mag....
emptus ab yuone de e'atest (?) eius oxon.

40. Postilla super Psalmos   xiii   ? Ely
 On fly-leaf. Psalterium glosatum (xiii)   caput libri *or* simi-
                                             litudinem
 Charter of Hugo de Northwold (1229): entries of lands at
Norwold.

41. Distinctiones Mauricii   xiv early   ? Lanthony
 Good border and initial.   Mark erased (?) at bottom of f. 1.
See Catalogue 191, 192.   di. q. homo

42. Marianus Scotus   xii   Abingdon
 Iste est liber lxxxviij in inuentario almarioli claustr°.
 Lumley.   Adjudged to Abingdon in view of insertions in
the text.

43. Ianuensis Sermones   xiv   sublimis

44. Augustinus in Joannem   xii   ? Lanthony
 Cat. 167 ?   bibebat quod

45. Isidori Etymologiae. Fine small
    hand   xii   ? Lanthony
    A Hebrew scribble on last fly-leaf.
    Cat. 473 ?   ad portum eterne

46. Clementines   Ireland 1477
    Written by Roderic Olacthnain, Prior of Fons Vini de
Lothra ordinis S. Augustini.
    Colophon in red at end.

47. Decretales   xiii   genitam

48. Higden Polychronicon   xiv
    The name Rawson in blue and gold, and in red, on fly-leaf.
                      annorum *or* scripta sunt

49. Durandi Repertorium etc.   xiv   St Aug. Cant.
    Repertorium Durandi. ❦. liber fratris Thome de Wyveles-
bergh de adquisicione. de librario S. Augustini Cant. D.
xvi. g. 4°.   et de differenciis
    Catalogue, f. 130.

50. Augustini tractatus   xv   Porro si

51. Petrus Londoniensis de Visionibus xiii   London (?)
    De vj^{to} ordine xlii^{us} : at bottom of f. 1.   experimentum *or*
    Lumley.   Arundel.   per eum uidebant

52. Mariale   xiv   Cogitaui *or* in-
                               *ter*ne cautus

53, 54. Paper, xvi.

55. Aristotelis Metaphysica   xiv   Lanthony
    Liber R. de Gloucestria Canonici
    Lanthon.   et architectores
    Cat. p. 214, note 3.

56. Gregorii Moralia   xii   ? Lanthony
    Fine round hand.   Cat. 415–17.   munerum

57. Epistolae Pauli sec. Longobar-
    dum   xiii   Lincoln Fran-
                              ciscans

fratrum minorum de Lincoln.   sibi mutauit
fratris Radulfi de Cortage.

58. S. Thomas super Quartum   xiv   Lanthony
     Liber Lanthon: iuxta Gloucestrie per   quam uile
     Will: priorem.

59. Anselmi Epistolae   xii & xv Chr. Ch. Cant.
     Title. Epistole Anselmi maiores. D. ii. g. x. Mark Γ.
                                              et amplector
     Lumley. Omitted accidentally by Edwards, but entered in
     the MS. of the Catalogue (Galba E. iv). It is also in Ingram's
     list, no. 145.

60. Johannes super sextum   xiii ? Dinsley Temple
                                                or Dingley
     Iste liber pertinet ad priorem de dyneleke   biterenmense

61. (1) Neckam super Psalterium   xiii   uɼm stat
     (2) Bulls: notes by Bale.   m̄unt et exigunt
     (3) Henr. de Hertley sermo de S. Thoma.
          Marked Bundle, 2. 5.

62. Ric. Pratellensis in Genesim   xii   Chr. Ch. Cant.
     Mark Ɔ÷.   minat sed
     Vol. ii. is at Trinity College, Cambridge, B. 3. 14.
     Edwards, p. 147.

63. Lombardus in Psalmos 'per R.
          Decani'   xii   Lanthony
     Psalt. mag. P. Lumbardi.   Liber Lanthonie iuxta Glouc.
     Cat. no. 51, 2.   uerba domini

64. Gregorii Registrum   xii   ? Exeter
     C on fly-leaf.   enim fluctus

65. Missal of Jean Aubépine, Bp of Limoges   1484
     Kershaw, p. 62.

66. Paper, xvi.

67. Boethii Arithmetica etc.   xii   Bury St Edm.
     Liber S. Aedmundi.   B. 318.
     Arithmetica boecii cum multis astronomie.

Musica eiusdem boecii.
Belonged to John Dee. His name is erased, but ' 1558 30
Junii Londini' remains. It is no. 167 in his Catalogue (ed.
Halliwell, Camd. Soc.).

68. Durandi Rationale : Italian initial xiv   Lanthony
    Given by John Leche.   non diligamus

69 Missal of Abp Chicheley   xiv   Chr. Ch. Cant.
    Kershaw, p. 31.

70. Burley super Porphyrium etc.   xiv   Lanthony
    Liber monasterii siue prioratus Lant. iuxta Glouc. emptus
    per fr. Ric. Calne...a.d. 1413.   rationi quidditatem

71. (1) Cantor in Psalmos   xiii   Lanthony
    Roberto Leckoford Canonico Lantoniensi.   spinas
    Cat. no. 53.

    (2) Langton in Isaiam   Lanthony
    Cat. no. 146.   egestionem

72. Legenda Aurea (Caxton) mut. init.   xv

73. (1) Will. Neubrigensis   xii   saris impium
    (2) Four Sermons, one on St Alban.
    (3) Pastor Hermae   meus in hoc
    ειμι βιβλιον Ταλβωτου και φιλοτεις.
    This is Robert Talbot, Prebendary of Norwich, the friend of
    Leland.

74. Burley in Aristotelem etc.   xiv   prime generalium
    'scriptus a.d. M°CCC°XCI°.'

75. Apocalypse, French   xiii   de asye
    Kershaw, p. 55.

76. (1) Aug. Retractationes etc.   xiii, xiv   Rochester
    Liber de claustro Roffensi per Laurentium de London.
    (2) Encheridion S. Aug. Aug. de spiritu et anima.
    Liber sentenciarum prosperi   sz apti

77. Ezechiel et Daniel glosati   xiii   Lanthony
    Cat. no. 14.   Ex preteritis

78. Speculum Parvulorum 1448   Chr. Ch. Cant.
    Liber compositus et perquisitus dompni W. Chartham
monachi huius ecclesie.   tam crucem

79. Summa Dumbleton   xiv   memorie plo^{nis}

80. (1) Hugutio. Bad hand   xiii   Lanthony
    Cat. 574.   dicitur cannula
    (2) Bernardus Papiensis xiii   adquisierit

81. Job et Daniel glosati. Fine initial xii   Lanthony
    Title. IOB ET DANIEL in red and black on fly-leaf.
    Cat. no. 15.   in summis *or* et erat

82. Pictaviensis summa   xiii   fuerit oportet

83. Historia Scholastica   xiii   Lanthony
    ...canonici Lanthon.   ciuit modo $\overline{\text{xpm}}$
    Cat. 260, 1.

84. Brute Chronicle in English with
    rough drawings   xv
    Kershaw, p. 41.

85. Libri Regum glossati   xii   Lanthony
    Title. LIBER REGUM as in no. 81.
    Cat. no. 28.

86. Homiliarium   xiv   ipse gestaret
    Hand like that of 38.

87. Pupilla Oculi etc.   xv   i. sacramenti
                     ii. anthicus in ueteri
    Pasted into the volume is a large and early copper engraving
of the Nativity, Adoration, etc.

88. Aug. contra Maximinum etc. xii   Lanthony
    Cat. no. 170.   net per se ipsum

89. Biblia.   xiv   epistolam
    Historiated initials.

90. Biblia   xiii   Bury St Edm.
    Title. Biblia integra Johannis Yxworth. 2. mea hoc
    Inscription at end: "Thys boke was put out to be lyned by

Stephen Edrych parson of Shatisham on to Master Hugh Candederby for the sum of xl^s....1384, after the deth of whych Stephen the saide booke came to the hands of one Mr John Yxworth sumtyme moncke of Bury," etc. It then passed to Roger Duckett, scholar at the Grammar School, Bury, who in 1573 gave it to Robert Chabenor.

91. Paper, xvii.

92. Bracton   xiii   Ely *or* Norwich
    Names occur of Nicholas Stewarde and Augustine Stewarde (Mayor of Norwich).

93. Bracton mut. utrinque   xiv   ? Lanthony
    Cat. p. 220, note 3.

94. Vitae Sanctorum   xiv   suo optimus

95. Aug. in Genesim   xiii   ? Lanthony
    Cat. no. 183, 4.   perfecta illa

96. (1)   Ebroicensis Epistola   xii & xi   ? Lanthony
    (2)   Gregorius in Ezechielem   mea ad eos
    Title.   Greg. super Ezech.   W. de folkyngham.
    (3)   Gregorii Homiliae xl   xii   Lanthony
    Iste liber constat ecclesie conuentuali Lanthon. prime in Wallia ex mutuo concedit decanus herford.
    Cat. no. 120.

97. S. Thomas in Metaphysica etc.   xiii   Lanthony
    Given by Richard Calne in 1415.   libro de anima

98. Paper, xvii.

99. Brute Chronicle
      Initials R. E.   xiv   onustas auro
      Rogerus Cestriensis.

100. Alexander in Aristotelem etc.   xv late   pō mālis

101. Cassiani Collationes   xiii   ? Lanthony
    Cat. no. 210.   institutione

102. Lucas et Johannes glosati.   Fine
      initials   xii, xiii   ? Lanthony
    Cat. no. 19.   Begins with the Gospel-Canons.   In montem

103. Decretals   xiii   Lanthony
Liber decretalium ecclesie b. marie Lanthonie iuxta
Gloucestr.
Cat. no. 235.

104. R. Higden Polychronicon etc.   xiv, xv percussa est in
Contains a Wheel of Fortune.

105. (1) Ric. Barre super Bibliam.
Large hand   xiii   Bury St Edm.
Liber Ricardi Barre super bibliam. R. 36.
(2) John Beleth. Extraordi-
narily small hand   xii
Supplement (xiv). Hunc librum scripsit philippus capel-
lanus cuius anima requiescat in pace amen.
(3) Innocent. Decretals   xiii   secundum varie-
tatem
Comment follows : one or two scribbles in Hebrew.

106. Cypriani Epistolae etc.   xii   Lanthony
Liber Lanthoniensis ecclesie : qui eum alienauerit ana-
thema sit.
Cat. no. 199.

107. Hugo de Folieto. Table in red
frame on fly-leaf   xii   Buildwas
Liber S. Marie de bildewas.

108. Acts in Slavonic. Paper.

109. Gregorii Moralia   xii   Buildwas
Liber S. Marie de bildewas.

110. Exodus glosatus   xiii   ? Lanthony
Cat. no. 26, 7.   addatur

111. Egidius in Aristotelem   xiv   ? Norwich
Title on fly-leaf and on f. 1, like those in Norwich books.
                                  si non est

112. Polychronicon   xiv   Lanthony
The name of Hugo de Lacy (founder of Lanthony) is on the
last leaf.   summariam *or* dicitur

113. Paper, xvi, xvii.

114. Libri Judicum etc. glosati   xiii   Lanthony
Cat. no. 20. Belongs to the same set as 110.
dictionem quia

115. Sententiae   xiv   Utrum debeat *or*
cum esse homines

116. (1) Brito etc.   xiii, xiv St Aug. Cant.
De libris S. Aug. Cant. Dist. Thome Abbatis.   Jordanis
Liber T. Abbatis. Cat. f. 13.
(2) Bromyard. Mut. init. Bad hand.

117. Gawain Douglas's Virgil. Paper, xvi.

118. Henry of Huntingdon   xii   Merton
Liber Wyke donatus per executores suos ecclesie.
b. marie merton in Com. Surr. (xvi).   ditum nostrum
Lumley.

119. Johannes Supprior in Apocalypsim (so title)   xiii   Lanthony
Cat. no. 130.   laborantes ecclesie

120. Hugutio   xiv   ? Bury
Iste liber est fratris Johannis Weysnham 1464. proaui pater
A Robert de Wesyngham occurs in a Bury MS. (Harley 51).
See my *Essay* on the Abbey of Bury, p. 53.

121. Armachanus. Paper, xv.   ideo videtur

122. P. Cantoris Verbum abbreviatum xiii   ? Lanthony
quantitatem
Cat. no. 157.   *or* statim

123–126. Paper, xvii.

127. I. de Abbatisvilla Sermones etc. xiii   deputata

128. Johannes super Sextum   xiv   Lanthony
Left by Nicholas Kaerwent.

129. Joh. Damasceni Sententiae etc. xiv   Lanthony
Left by John Leche.

130. Matthaeus glosatus   xii   ysaac autem

131. Brute Chronicle. Paper.

132. Mauricii Distinctiones   xiv   ? Lanthony
     Initial and border.   ad laborem

133. Hubertus super Regulam S.
     Augustini   xiv   ? Lanthony
     Cat. no. 478 ?   in contemplacione

134. (1) Isaias glosatus   xii   ? Lanthony
                              trinitatem
     Cat. no. 21 ?   or dicit dominus
     (2) Jeremias glosatus   xiii   uerba or tum est

135. Vita S. Thomae etc.   xiii   etiam assessorum
     Lumley.

136. Epistolae S. Thomae   xii   comitem or
                              ne punienda

137. Bartholomaeus de proprietatibus
     rerum   xiv   nulla notio

138. Seneca   xiii   ? Lanthony
     ' Bundle, 2. 7.'   ut de ratione
     The rest paper, including Vita Edwardi and Vita Thomae.

139. (1) Regulae Juris etc.   xiii   empcionem
                              inicē ultra
     (2) Liber iste est m. arnulfi quem N. capellanus dedit
         illi.

140. Paper, xvi, xvii.

141. Aug. de Trinitate. Title on p. 1.   xiii   ? Exeter
     C on fly-leaf.   nituntur

142. (1) Pictavensis summa etc.   xiii, xiv   nec conuennit
     (2)   xiv   totum humanum

     (3) Unum ex quatuor. Alex-
          andri de Hospreng   xiii   Chr. Ch. Cant.
     D. ii. G. xii^{us}. Edwards, p. 202.   notatur

143. Burley. Paper and vellum.

144. (1) Gregorii Pastoralis etc. xiv S. Aug. Cant.
Di. VIII. gradu v°. sunt admirentur
Collectiones Tbome de Cirencestria. Liber S. Aug. Cant.
At end : Liber Thome Cyrencestria quem dedit ecclesie S.
Aug. Cant. pro animabus patris et matris sue et omnium
fidelium defunctorum. Cat. f. 115.

   (2) Gregorius in Ezechielem xii in eo lamenta-
Like Christ Church hand. tiones

145. (1) Ps. Chrysostomi opus imperfectum etc. xv Lanthony
From Richard Calne ' tempore quo fuit scolaris oxonie.'

   (2) Chrysostomus de Peniten-
tia etc. xii Croyland
Inscription partly erased : liber iste de armariolo Croylondie
......a.d. M. CC. septuag......librum qui vocatur C......S. iosephi
......de mirabilibus mundi pro memoriali.
Also : liber Croylondie.
Bundle, 2. 8.

146. Ambrosius super Lucam xii ? Lanthony
Cat. no. 122. de publicano or
storum domini

147. (1) Beda super Parabolas xii Lesnes
In red : hic liber est ecclesie b. marie de liesnes etc.
Hand very like Christ Church : an odd panelled initial in
red and green.

   (2) Beda super Marcum xii ? Lanthony
Good initial. Cf. Cat. no. 136. uocatur

148. (1) Beda super Genesim xii Lanthony
tas cum

   (2) Albinus super Genesim. Late title on last page :
In isto uol. continentur.

149. (1) Beda super Apocalypsim x, xi transitus
Chain-mark at bottom of f. 1.
Aug. de adulterinis coniugiis etc. x, xi Crediton (Exeter)

f. 138. Given by Æthelward to St Mary's Church at......
(name obliterated by galls: see Preface) in 1018.

On the same page is:
    † æþel † æþelperd ealdorman gret.

And in green capitals:
    A: IN NOMINE DOMINI. AM*en*.
    LEOFRIC*us* PATER.

(2) Aug. Enchiridion etc.	xii	Lanthony
Title at top of fly-leaf cut off.		quod remissio
Cf. Cat. 186.		*or* autem ab alio

150. Aegidius de Regimine Princi-
pum etc.   xv   Lanthony
From John Leche.

151. Aug. et anselmi tractatus   xiii   Lanth. *or* Glouc.
Iste liber est de (*erasure*: ? ecclesia Lanth. iuxta) Glouc.'
Vol. 2 in a large xiii[th] cent. hand.

152. Gregorii moralia   xii, xiii   ? Lanthony
Cat. no. 45–7.   uel etiam

153. (1) Isaias glosatus	xii	Lanthony
xv[th] cent. title. Cat. 33–35, 71.		sacrificiis
(2) Gospels: fine large hand	xii	genuit ioatham
(3) Lucas glosatus	xiii	? Lanthony

xv[th] cent. title. In isto uol. continetur lucas glosatus.
           Item diuersi sermones cum aliis, etc.

154. Exodus glosatus   xii   Lanthony
Liber mag. philippi de sancto breauel.
Cat. no. 26, 7.

155. Paper, xvi.

156. Historia scholastica   xiv   tenebre vnde
Rob. Hare 1566.
At end a Cautio of 1488.

157. xvi.

158. Armachanus   xiv   auctoris qui

159. Vitae Sanctorum (controversy
about S. Dunstan), paper and
vellum   xvi   Chr. Ch. Cant.
Liber d. Jacobi Hartey monachi ecclesie Christi Cant.
Later names: Will. Hadley, John Sarysbury, Ric. Hatton.

160. Polychronicon. Good ornaments. xiv   Franciscan
Memoriale fr. Willelmi broscumbe magistri.   K. ij.
I. Winterus (xvi).   contra nature

161. Bernardus super Cantica   xiii   ex dignitate
                                   or eorum legitur

162. Repertorium Bibliae (paper)   xv

163. Vita S. Bernardi   xiv   dei domum suam
On fly-leaf: Alwoldesle Cathedralium.
Lumley.

164. Epistolae Pauli sec. Anselmum   xii   ? Lanthony
Title on fly-leaf. Cat. no. 155, 6.   dilectis

165. (1) Canones Poenitentiales   xii, xiii   Lanthony
      (2) Homiliae   xii   nocentem cum
Title as in no. 153 and the name Morganus canonicus de
Kermerd.   prudentiam

166. Legal   xiv

167. Paper, xvi.

168. Ockam. Paper and vellum   xv

169. Bradwardine de causa dei   xiv   bonum et malum
Title (xv) at top of f. 1.   *or* vel si oporteat
Lumley.

170. Psalterium glosatum. Good out-
line initial   xii early   Lanthony
Cat. no. 48 sqq.   eos et dominus

171. Constitutions   xiv   accepta a sacer-
                                       dote

172. Concordance   xiv

Has two letters of fraternity to Giles Tylor and Christina his wife,

    (1)   From Austin Friars.   Salopie, 1383.

    (2)   From Carmelites.   Bristol, 1382.

173. Egesippus   xi   ? Lanthony

    Visiones.   sue successorem

    Names : master dan Thomas hobyll.

           Euerard.

    Cat. no. 129.

174. Petrus de Crescentiis 1440   est ne sit

    Edo. Orwell, 1586.

175.

176. (1)   Petrus Comestor sermones   xiii   Lanthony

    Cat. no. 145.   hunc modum

    (2)   Io. Beleth.   asinam

    (3)   Comm. in Psalmos.   his ut uerba

    (4)   ,,   ,,   ,,   que carnaliter

177, 8.   Paper, xv, xvi.

179. (1)   Henry of Huntingdon etc.   xiii   sit britannia

                                          or diuisa

    (2)   Statutes   xv

    (3)   Paper, xvi.

180. Russel in Cantica etc.   xiv   ? Chr. Ch. Cant.

    Postille super cantica fr. Thome Stoyl.   h^i ille

    T. Stoyl was monk of Chr. Ch.: see Defectus librorum, 1337.

181. Polychronicon   xiv   bique et per

    Liber Th. dakecomb 1550.

182. (1, 2) Paper, xvi.

    (3)   De penetentiis et remissionibus : Bundle 2. 4. 4.

    (4)   Expositio Gallice in orat. Dominica : Bundle 2. 4. 1.

183. Chronica T. Rudborne.   Paper, xv.

184. Egidius de Regimine Princi-
        pum etc.   late xv   Westminster
  I. Foxus. Has arms of Westminster Abbey.   et grosse

185. Hildeberti Sermones   xii   St Aug. Cant.
      Liber S. Aug. Cant. Sermones Noui Abbatis Rogerii D.
      VIII. G. II. Cat. f. 49.   claudi erant

186. Psalter   late xv
      Kershaw, p. 42.

187. Bernardus super Cantica   xii   ? Lanthony
      Cat. no. 140. Odd initials.   oris sui

188. Flores Historiarum   xiv   sec. lxx. inter-
      A few leaves in the middle are of cent. xiii.   pretes

189. Hugo de Sacramentis   xiii   Lanthony
      Liber lanthoniensis ecclesie. Cat. no. 217, 18.

190. (1) Biblia.   xiv   hanc garula
      (2) Brito.   ? Lanthony

191. Beda super Parabolas. mut. init. xii   debriare
      Bundle 2. 10. Cf. Cat. no. 345.

192. (1) Rebot Historia Carmeli-
            tarum. Belonged to Bale xv   monachorum
      (2) The same in English.   xv
      Liber Johannis Caw.

193. Ordinale Carmelitarum   xv   quando ut

194. De Sedacione Schismatis   xv   Chr. Ch. Cant.
      Liber ecclesie x̅p̅i Cant. (xv).   tuor sunt
      Ingram, no. 172.

195. Priscian. xv^{th} cent. title   xii   Lanthony
      Liber ? lanthoniensis ecclesie ex dono gaufredi   gl'aribus
      Meneuensis episcopi. Cat. no. 372.

196. Priscian   xi, xii   Lanthony
      Liber Lanthonie iuxta Gloucest'. Cat. no. 371 etc.
                                                Philosophi

A rhyming poem on the fly-leaves, beginning :
In aspectam nube tectam
sero arthon intuens.
Dum mirarer et testarer
nubes esse renuens.

197. Psalterium glosatum   xii   ? Lanthony
Cat. no. 48 sqq. Very odd rude pale initials.   astiterunt

198, 198b. Consuetudines Petrobur- xiv, xv Peterborough
genses of Abbot Richard Ashton. Written by
John Trentham.

199. Historia Bibliae   xii   uitulos
Sententiae etc.   or desperaui

200. (1) Bacon, paper   xv
     (2) Aldhelm. Kershaw, p. 29.   Waltham
        Front. to Todd's *Cata-*
        logue. Waltham mark,
        cxxx al. ca.   ? ix   dante
     (3) Distinctiones super Psalte-
        rium etc.   xiii   Lanthony
xv[th] cent. title. Above, in pencil :
    Iste liber est de......prioris lanthonie prime.
On the fly-leaf is a note on king Anna.
A Litany has Kyneburga (of Gloucester).

201. Aug. in Genesim   xiii   ? Lanthony
    tendit

202. Aug. Sermones etc.   xii, xiii   deus pater
Contemporary table headed :
Isti sunt libri quos corpus continet istud.

203. Aug. Confessions etc.   xii, xiii   Exeter
    Damus ecclesie nostre Exon. quia multum laboraui in
corrigendo. J. Exon. (Grandison.)
    On f. 118 : Ego J. de G. scripsi hec dum studerem parisiis,
and other like notes.

204. Gregorii Dialogi etc.   x   ? Ely
Interlaced work in initials: minuscule hand: heading in
capitals.
At end: Ða æfter æadgares cininges ford side on ðam
geþalce.
On the last leaf a wheel in yellow.
Arms of Robert Stewarde, last Prior of Ely.

205. Bartholomaeus de Casibus   xiv   ab excommuni-
Scribbles at end, and some macaronic verses.   catione

206. (1) Comm. in Matthaeum   xv late   celesti
John Aleyn de Oxbourgh on fly-leaf at end.
   (2) Io. de Rupella   xiii   ip(s)e est
Vnde malum. Roberti de Hol. Senior.

207. Epistolae Pauli glosatae. Good
       outline initials   xii   Lesnes
Liber ecclesie b. Thome martiris de liesnes.   gratie uobis

208. Isaias glosatus   xii   Lanthony
                                          visio *or* ceram
xv^{th} cent. title. Morganus canon de Kermerd.

209. Apocalypse, pictured   xiii
Lumley.
Kershaw, p. 47.
Pal. Soc. It contains the picture and arms of a Lady de
Quincey: probably executed at Canterbury. At the end are
full-page paintings of the Life of St John, the Story of Theo-
philus, and various saints.

210. Baldewini opera   xii, xiii   Jervaux
At end: liber sancte marie Joreuallis.   tio ut res

211. Th. Bekynton Epistolae   xv late   Wells
                                                   cessionis

212. Nic. de Clemangiis   xv late   cure sue
Lumley. The fly-leaf is a document.

213. Missal   xiv   ? Irish
Masses of SS. Finnan, David, Chad, etc. at end.

214. Aug. tractatus. Several volumes.

       xivth cent. table   xii, xiii, xiv   Ely

At end: Inquisitio jurisdictionis prioratus de Ely in Chatteris etc.   tacionibus

215. Athanasius de Trinitate   xii, xiii   Lanthony
      xvth cent. title. Memoriale de Lanthonia.
      Cat. no. 111.

216. Oculus sacerdotum   xiv   ? Lanthony
      Cat. p. 212, note 3. P. Laur. at end.   penitentiam

217. (1) Iob glosatus   xii   Lanthony
      Cat. no. 66.   deus ait

     (2) Iob glosatus, fragment   xii   Lanthony
      Cat. no. 67 ?   quadam

     (3) Matheus imperfectus [et
            Johannes glosatus in ·1·
            volumine]   xii   Lanthony
      De v^{to} gradu primi armarii. Cat. no. 16, 85.   autem
                                     genuit

     (4) Pauli Epistolae   xii   ē fidem

218. (1) Gregorii Pastoralis   xii   Lanthony
      xvth cent. title. Cat. no. 124, 5.   necessitas

     (2) Cassiani Collationes   xiv   Bury St Edm.
      Liber S. Edmundi Regis in quo continentur   I. 23
      Ioh. Cassianus de septem collacionibus patrum.

     (3) Alcuini Epistolae   ix   Bury St Edm.
      Mut. init. Title (xiv) written on 1st page of erased text.

On the fly-leaf of the Cassian is   gratiarum
E. 43. Epistole Albyni siue Alcuyni.

On the same leaf (recto) and in the same hand is a paragraph beginning:

Vir illustris et facundus Johannes Cassianus multa scripsit utilia inter que patrum antiquorum regulas et instituta et xxiiii^{or} collaciones eorundem conscripsit que certe opuscula multam edificacionem, etc.

At the end is a statement about the reading of the Collations 'ut habetur in regula ca.° xlii° et ca. lxxiii°.'

Vide originalia xxiiii collacionum patrum in registro librorum
in J. 35.

219. Gislebertus in Psalterium. Fine
     initial to Ps. i   xii   ?Lanthony
At top of f. 1 psalterium Gileberti uniuersalis.   contra
Small hand of Christ Church type.   Cat. no. 54.   eum

220. Lucas glosatus   xiii   ?Lanthony
     Cat. no. 33–5.   vbi domino *or* deum
                          secundum

221. Tabula Coldrini etc.   xv   Exeter *or* Ottery
Table to Holkot signed ' hec orum.'
Will of John Grandison, followed by a note on his foundation
of Ottery St Mary.
     Sermons xiv and xv in many hands.
     Letters, f. 262 sqq., paper. Lumley.

222. Legenda Aurea   xiv   Crich
Per manus Willelmi de Weston vicarii de Crych.   retro
Rich. Hauk, Vicar of Crich, gives the book to the parish.

223. Golden Legend in English verse   xiv
Written by R. W. of þis toun. To a gode man of þe same is
cleped Thomas of Wottoun.
     Johannes Raynscroft.

224. Anselmi opera   xii   quod hec *or*
Written by William of Malmesbury.   bonus equus
Inscription (xv): Liber M. T. Stevynson ex dono M. J.
Mersham cuius anime deus propicietur.
     Liber m. rowlandi philipp. vicarii de croydon.
     At top of original table of contents:
          Disputat anselmus presul cantorbiriensis
          Scribit willelmus monachus malmesberiensis
          Ambos gratifice complectere lector amice.
     At the top of f. 1 of text: ·xxvj·
     On fly-leaves at end Cautiones: one of xiii^s iiij^d ciste uni-
uersitatis.

225, 6. Paper, xvi, xvii.

227. Comm. in Psalmos (Egredimini)   xii, xiii   Lanthony
    xvth cent. title. Cat. no. 48 etc.   prophetie

228. Matthaeus glosatus   xii, xiii   Lanthony
    Cat. no. 41–44.   In nullo *or* natus

229. Matthaeus glosatus   xiii   Lanthony
    Cat. no. 41–44.   id in terram
                                  or liber

230. Matthaeus glosatus   xiii   Lanthony
    Cat. no. 41–44. Erasure on fly-leaf.   hic est *or* cui
                                  prima

231. Matthaeus glosatus   xii   Lanthony
    xvth cent. title. Morganus canon. de Kermerd.   liber
    Cat. no. 41–44.

232. Seneca de Beneficiis: de Cle-
       mentia   xii   non est
    Erasure on fly-leaf.

233. Psalter. Exceedingly fine   xiv
    The blank page following Kalendar has in pencil
    Memento mei domine quod J. Rowham.

At the bottom of f. 1 of text are just such grotesques as in the Morris MS. at the Fitzwilliam Museum (no. 242).

There are armorial line-fillings. Those of commonest occurrence are:

(1) checky of *arg.* and *gu.* (2) *az.* cinqfoils *or.* (3) *gu.* 3 lions *or.* (4) *gu.* 3 butterflies (?) *arg.* (5) chequers *or* and *az.* (6) *az.* two bends sinister *arg.*

Exaudi domine (ci) has a crowned man kneeling at an altar. In the spandrels are arms: *arg.* 2 chevrons *az.* in chief 2 bezants *gu.*

Dixit dominus is cut out.

Ad dominum (cxix). A lady kneeling. Arms in the spandrels *arg.* 2 fesses *gu.* in chief 3 bezants of the second.

The Kalendar in French, in blue, red, and gold.

Feb. S. William Conf.

Mar. Patrice, Edward, Cuthbert.

Ap. Richard, Alphege, Wlfrid euesk de Beue*r*lee.

June 7. Seint Will'. de euerewyk.

    9. Transl. de S. Edmund le erceueske.

    10. Transl. S. emund C*a*ntu.

Botolf. Transl. of Edward k. m., Paulin, Etheldred.

Oct. 6. Transl. S. hue de Nich' (= Lincoln).

    Wlfrid euesk, fredeswide.

Nov. emoun erceueske, Edmoun roy e. martir.

Kershaw, p. 56.

234. Paper, xvi.

235. John Beleth, etc.   xiii   ? Lanthony
    Cat. no. 299. Contemporary table.   de cellula

236. Giraldus Cambrensis   xiii   quemadmodum
    Contents in red. On f. 3 in blue:
    Giraldus meneuensis archidiaconus clericis et officialibus suis.

237. (1) Aug. contra Manicheos   xii   nol$\overline{\text{t}}$ n^{i} eos
    (2) Gregory Nyssen   xiii   one in mani-
                               festatione
    (3) Aug. in 1 Johannis etc.   xiii   ? Lanthony
    ' Bundle 2. 4. 2. 3.'
    (4) Encheiridion Aug. etc. '*En-*
           cheridion ' (xiii) on f. 1 x   quod peccatum
           Sextus Pythagoræus.   *or* Haec sunt
    Drawing of a horseman on a fly-leaf at end.

238. Laurentius Dunelmensis etc.   xii, xiii   ? Lanthony
    Title ' megacosmus ' in Lanthony hand ?   perantia
    Senatus Bravonius (of Worcester) on the Mass occurs at
    p. 207.

239. Clemens Lanthoniensis in vii
        Epp. Canonicas   xiii   Lanthony
    Erasure on fly-leaf, ending ' Lant.'   iuxta
    Cat. no. 109.   *or* consilium

240. Gregorius super Ezechielem   xii   ? Lanthony
    Title: Greg. super Ezechielem.   tangit ex

241. Register of Dover Priory   xiv   Dover

242, 3. Canterbury Accounts. xiii, xiv Chr. Ch. Cant.

244. Register of Abp. Robert Winchelsey.

245–252. Paper, xvi–xvii.

253. Historia Scholastica. Mut. init. xii, xiii

254. Lydgates Bochas. xv

255–260. Paper.

261. Barlaam and Josaphat, etc. xiii Newstead
Liber S. Marie de nouo loco in Schirewod : also twice at the end.

262–297. Paper, and late. 265. Dicta of Philosophers xv, belonged to Edward IV (?). Kershaw, p. 38.

298. Sydrac xiii e cheque
Well written.

299–302. Paper.

303. Gervasii Cantuar. Chronicon. xv Chr. Ch. Cant.
Cronica de archiepiscopis Stephani Byrchinton Monachi ecclesie xp̄i Cantuar. possessiones
Belonged to Laud. Original binding : strap and pin.

304–324. Paper. 323. Jura et Privilegia (Laud) : Kershaw, p. 77.

325. Ennodius x Durham
Title : Ennodius I^a 7. Θ. quisque uinceret.
Catt. Vett. p. 32. A. Ennodius. 2 fo. quisque uinceret.
J. Foxus. On the fly-leaf are some names of monks and Parce michi domine, etc.

326. Pilgrimage of the Soul in Latin,
with pictures xv ora est
Fine French initials : good book-desks in the 2nd and 3rd pictures.

327. Henry of Huntingdon xii, xiii crisippus

328. Mirror of Life of Christ xv

3—2

329. Nic. de aquavilla Sermones   xv   oculos
     Ex dono Reuerendi dompni Johannis danyell prioris tali
     condicione ut ex eo usum habeat quamdiu uixerit.

330. Valerii Epistola cum commento.
     Good ornament   xiv, xv   tunt et i*deo*
     Thomas Bemound (xvi).

331–3. xv, xvi.

334. Lectionary. Mut. init. Fine
     hand   xii

335. (1) Proverbia glosata   xii, xiii   ? Lanthony
                                      quod timebatis
      (2) Cantica etc. glosata   xiii   Lanthony
     De primo armario 4^{ti} gradus.
      (3) Epistolae Catholicae. Ugly xii, xiii   ? Lanthony
     Cf. Cat. nos. 84, 208, 200.   ut sitis

336. Aug. Confessions   xii   continendo

337. Aug. Retractations etc.   xii   ? Lanthony
     Contemporary table : In hoc uol. continentur.   originali
     Cat. no. 187.   *or* cum diuersa

338. (1) Gregory Nazianzen   xii   ? Lanthony
     (Cena Rabani).   sue abscessionis
                                    or scandalum
      (2) Leonis Sermones etc.   xii   itaque mensis
     Hec est continentia huius uol.   Erased.
     Cat. no. 295.

339. Porphyrii Isagoge etc. Good.   . xii   Lanthony
     On the last page in capitals : liber Lanthonie iuxta Glou-
     cestriam.
        On fly-leaf (xiii).   Ysagoge porfirii
                       Predicamenta aristotil :
        Cat. no. 312.

340. Chronica   xv   pulcherrimo
     On f. 1 (xvi).   Gul. de. R. Le. to.
                 J. N. (Also in no. 222.)

341. Petrus de Monte etc. Two
    narrow columns   xv   codices
xvth cent. title, but, I think, not from Lanthony.
Rob. Hare 1576.

342. (1) Cicero de Officiis   xiii   ?Lanthony
? Cat. no. 357. Q. Tullius de officiis.   colendum
    (2) Fly-leaf xv in the Bury
        hand. Many hands   xii–xiv magis intuerer
Contenta in hoc libro sunt ista :
    1. Sompnium publii cornelii scipionis.
    2. Macrobius super sompnium scipionis.
    3. Mixtologia fabularum fulgencii.
    4. Enigmata symphosii.
    5. Cronica locorum habitabilium et temporum.
    6. Tractatus de spiritu Guidonis.
    7. Gesta Regis Alexandri.
Ex dono M^{ri} Rogeri Marchall.
This part is bound in a deed about a Preceptory of the
Knights Templars.
Roger Marchall gave books to Peterhouse, Gonville and
Caius, and other places.

343. Deuteronomium et Josue glosati.
    Original binding   xii, xiii   Lanthony
On fly-leaf in black and red DEVTERONOMIUM ET IOSVE.
Cat. no. 22.

344. Lydgate   xv

345. (1) Gregorii Homiliae etc.   xii, xiii   Lanthony
    (2) Registrum Gregorii   xii   (in libro) et grex
xvth cent. title. Cat. no. 118.   ta est

346. Joh. Cassiani Regula. Original
    binding   xii   Lanthony
On last cover : HYERIVS · ROMANVS · ORATOR·   fidem

347. Will. Antissiodorensis in Senten-
    tias   xiii   liberalitatis
Nic. Trevet in Sententias.

348. Biblia   xiii   inspexeris
Anth. Higgin ex dono M. Nettleton 1592.

349. Genesis glosata. Original bind-
            ing   xii   ?Lanthony
Cat. nos. 29, 30. ¶ GENESIS on fly-leaf in black.   aquas

350. Registrum Brevium   xiv
Old binding.

351. Decreta: round hand   xi   ueniatur
Interpretationes nominum : Abana.

352. Visiones etc.   xiv   All Hallows the Great, Lond.
                                                perseuerabat
Pertinet liber iste M^{ro} Joh^i May rectori ecclesie omnium
sanctorum maioris London. ex dono d^{ni} Robert de Norton
capellani in Abbathia de Mallyng in com. Kancie.

353. Anselm etc.   xiii   Waltham
Mark: cxli. al. ca.
Crux sibi sancta librum de Waltham vendicat istum
quem qui furatur anathemate percuciatur.

354. Petrus de Monte etc.   xv   etiam ysaac
Edward Taylor.

355. Ivonis Chronicon   xiii   Bristol
Liber S. Aug. de Bristoll.   cere si quidem
Tho. Cant. (Cranmer). Lumley.

356. (1) Hieronymi Epistolae   xii   Lanthony
xvth cent. title. Cat. no. 116.   precidat
      (2) Hieron. ad Damasum   xii, xiii   vindicta
      (3) Petrus Manducator   xiii   libris
      (4) Anselm   xii   credamus

357. Hampole etc.   xiv   qui illam
Joh. Batte (xvi) at end.

358. Berengaudus in Apocalypsim   xii   libet propheta
Greek alphabet on fly-leaf.
At end : 'perscripto libro reddatur gloria Christo,' partly in
Runic letters.

359. Berengaudus in Apocalypsim.
    Mut. init.   xi, xii   significant
Rude frontispiece.   On fly-leaf BARINGVEDUS super apoca-
lipsim.

360. (1) Notae super Psalmos etc.
    Many hands   xii, xiii   Lanthony
xvth cent. title. At end (f. 118): Morganus canon. de
Kermerd: and a. d. millesimo quadringentesimo sexagesimo
Johannes Walsch.
    (2) Injunctions of Bp. Russel   1483   Peterborough

361. Hieronymus contra Jovinianum
    etc. Two volumes   xv   (1) caput
  At end of Vol. I (f. 56 b)   (2) gelii
    Item de magnis literis prec. ii^{d}.
    Item de paraffis iiiclxxxvj prec. viij^{d}.
  Vol. II is later: at end: Jo. Estmond. prec. ij^{s}.

362. Abbonis Vita S. Edmundi   xi, xvi ?Bury St Edm.
    Lumley.   deuotio

363. Isidore etc.   xii, xiii   ?Lanthony
    Old table on fly-leaf.   Cat. no. 149.   insueta

364. Cassiodorii Varia   xiii   ? Exeter
    Scribbles (xiv) 'de Poltemore' occurs often.   edere
    At end, in red: Finito libro reddatur cena Willelmo.
    Poltimore is 4 miles from Exeter.

365. (1) Aug. Confessions   xii early   Lanthony
    xvth cent. title. Cat. no. 174.
    (2) Aug. de doctrina Christiana
        etc.   xii, xiii   Lanthony
  Cat. no. 177 ?   aliquod

366. Innocentius de Missa   xii   de stola
    Contemporary table on fly-leaf.

367. Sententiae P. Lombardi   xiii   aut contrarium
    Erasure on fly-leaf. At end (xv):
    Constat m. heur. morcotte.

368. Psalter, Kershaw, p. 46   xiii
      Rough English work : a large Veronica-head before Ps. cix.

369. Wycliffite.

370. Questiones in Sententias. Old
           binding   xv   ? sumpcionem
      At end : Amen. Thomas Korn.

371. Imago Mundi etc.   xiii   Reading
      Old table of contents. Reading documents at the beginning.
      Ed. Orwell 1577.

372. Aug. de Fide et Symbolo   xiii   ? Lanthony
      Cat. no. 171.   rie mandanda

373. Smaragdus etc.   xi, xii   ? Lanthony
      Table and Capitula (xiv).   orare
      Fly-leaf (xv) : C (?) ·xvj
           Inc. liber de diademate monachorum cum aliis.
      Cat. no. 300.

374. Paper, xvi, xvii.

375. Albertanus Brixiensis   xiv   Lanthony
      From John Leche.

376. Anon. de Virtutibus. Old bind-   ? Lanthony
           ing   xiii   prudentie
      Cat. no. 298.

377. Isidore de summo bono. Caro-
           lingian minuscule   x   Lanthony
      xv^th cent. title. Cat. no. 143.   ab ipsa

378. (1) Alcuinus de Virtutibus et
                Vitiis   xii   Lanthony
      xv^th cent. title. Cat. no. 370.   ex toto
      (2) Ambrosii Exameron. Good
                initials : small hand xii   Lanthony
      Cf. Cat. p. 217, note 4.   ex lege

379. Brute   xii   in ipsis
      Stimulus amoris   xv   sanguis

380. (1) Isidore de summo bono etc.   xii   Lanthony
                                                lapsus
     (2) Isidore de Ecclesiasticis
           officiis   xii   Lanthony
     Liber Lantonie : old table on fly-leaf.
     Cat. no. 149.

381. Mauricii Distinctiones   xiv   ? Lanthony
     Cf. Cat. no. 191, 2.   abicietur

382. Dionysius Areopagita : fine hand xiii   poribus pape
     In three columns headed *vetus, nova, extracta.*
     At bottom of f. 1 the mark : I. xviij·
     At the end a leaf of a large x[th] cent. MS. in Carolingian
     minuscule.

383. Paper, xvi.

384. Albertanus Brixiensis   xiv   et irato
     Good frontispiece with arms, defaced.

385. Lucas glosatus   xii   ? Lanthony
     Cat. no. 33–5.   deum et deus
                                              or spiritu sancto

386. Chronica   xvi

387. Marcus glosatus   xii   ? Lanthony
     Cat. no. 32.   quam in

388. Sermones Dominicales   xiii   tellige
     Old table on fly-leaf.

389. (1) Interpretationes nominum
                Hebr.   xiii   ? Lanthony
     Cat. no. 91.   mem peccatum
     (2) Glossarium.

390. (1) Summa de Vitiis   xiii   Lanthony
     xv[th] cent. title.   Cat. no 289.   sequitur
     (2) Cantor. Concordance.

391. Sermons. (*Dicite pusillanimes*) xii, xiii   Lanthony
     Liber Lanthonie iuxta Gloucestriam.
     Cat. no. 215.

392. Pharetra Sacramenti and other   xii–xv
    tracts. Paper and vellum, in-
    cluding
    Qui bene presunt   xii   Lanthony
    Cat. no. 302, 3.   s^i uirgo

393. Penbygull Universalia etc.   xv   Lanthony
    Liber Lanthonie. Ricardi Calne.

394. (1) Innocentius de Missa   xiii   Lanthony
    xvth cent. title. Cat. no. 216.   h^i nunc
    (2) Questiones.

395. Hester etc. glosati. Several
    volumes   xii, xiii   Lanthony
    Cat. no. 38.   argentei

396. Questiones in Physica   xv   Lanthony
    ' partim scripsit partim scribi fecit Ric. Calne.'

397. Ailredi speculum caritatis   xii   Lanthony
    xvth cent. title.   habitu

398. (1) Sermons etc.   xiii   Lanthony
    xvth cent. title.   naan ·i·
    (2) Summa Raymundi
    Cat. no. 304–6.

399. Summa Raymundi etc.   xiii   inspexerit
    Summa Raymundi Nicholai de Iuyngho (xiii–xiv),
and : Nich. de Iuingho emit pro x^s de feretro beati T. martiris.

400. Sententiae P. Lombardi   xiv   quod deus
    Will^s de Kyrkele.   or qui deo

401. Dares etc.   xiii, xiv   ?Irish
    Scribbles at end. List of Irish counties.   collaudatus
    Nicholaus Locke (xvi).

402. Paper, xvii.

403. Brito de legibus   xiv   ne pasent

404. Decretals : red skin over boards   xiii, xiv   causam q^{a}ae
    Old title (xiii ?) on fly-leaf.

405–7. Paper, xvi, xvii.

408. (1) Sermons (York) in English xiv   so as
    (2) Sermons (ante diem festum) xiii   ? Lanthony
    Very small hand. Cat. p. 211, note 2.   videns

409. Medica: two volumes, fine hand xiii   Lanthony
    (1) On f. 1 : vii quaterni ii°.   intensa
    (2) xiv early : marked ii quaterni iii°.
On the last page a table signed : Morganus Canon. de
Kermerd.

410. Aug. Sermons (Eadmer)   xiv   Henton
On fly-leaf, stuck down : Iste liber est de domo loci dei de
Hentone ordinis Carthusie.   et rubicundum

411. Anon in Decreta. (*Operis cuius-*
    libet)   xiii   ut in duobus

412. Speculum sacerdotis   1458   Irish
The hand looks earlier than the date.
Colophon : Finit amen finit qui scripsit me mala morte
peribit. Scriptus et finitus est liber iste per edmundum
Ochomayn domino donaldo Okahvyll in ecclesia de Korcoteny
a. d. m°. c°c°c°c°. lviij°. mense decembri in die veneris proximo
post festum S. Thome apostoli. quorum animabus propicietur
deus.

413. Carthusian statutes. Paper, xv.

414. Excerpta Augustini etc. (Victo-
    rinus)   ix   St Aug. Cant.
    D. IIII. Gr. III.   quando quidem
    Liber S. Aug. Cant.
    Cat. f. 109.

415. Epistolae Honorii Prioris   xiii   Chr. Ch. Cant.
    Title EPISTOLE REGINALDI · DE · TEMPORE · BALDW(INI).
    D. iii. G. xiii^{us}. de prima demonstracione,
and :   De claustro x^i cant.
    Beaufoy. Thomas Draper. Edwards, p. 137.
    Edited by Dr Stubbs in the Rolls Series.

416–18. Paper, xvi, xvii.

419. Chronica   xiv   St Aug. Cant.
    Chronica de tempore Will. bastardi de librario S. Aug. Cant.
    Dist. x. G. 3.   pretendit nec
    Cat. f. 63.

420. Mariale etc., fine hand   xii   Hertford
    At bottom of f. 1 in red: Hunc librum dedit dominus
Johannes .ij. abbas de S. Albano ecclesie b. marie de herteford.
quem qui ei abstulerit anathema sit.

421. Petrus Blesensis. Fine hand   xiii   ? Lanthony
    Cat. no. 203.   tum est quia

422. Registrum Brevium   xiv   custodia
    Names at end (xv): Ridge Edward, Thoˢ Hall, Humfredus
Tendall, Nicholas Hantersvell, Laurentius Newton (?).

423. (1) Aristotle   xiii   pⁱius vᵒde
    (2) Priscian.
    Labyrinth on fly-leaf. On f. 1: priscianus minor.   natus

424. Paper, xvi.

425. (1) Cicero   xv & xiii non commo-
                               veri
    (2) Cicero de senectute. Large
         hand   xiii   de senectute
    (3) Paper, xvi.
    (4) Palladius   xii   Norwich or Ely
    1551 Augustinus Seneschallus (Stewarde, Mayor of Norwich)
me possidet. With sketch of arms.   ceris

426 = 1112. Paper, xvi.

427. Psalter with English gloss   ? x, xi   Lanthony
    On f. 209 b is written (xii ?) xᶜᵉᵐ P. Lanthonie.   quare
    On 2 ff. at end is a Saxon fragment on SS. Mildred,
Etheldreda, Sexburga, etc. See Cockayne, *Saxon Leechdoms*
iii. 428.
    There is a Litany of cent. xiv in two columns:
    Martyrs: Marcelle, Austremoni, Marine...Marcelle, Quin-
tine, Aedmunde, Olaue, Albane...Fortunate.

Confessors: Taurine, Augustine, Flore, Augustine, Dunstane, Cuthberte, Aedmunde, Benedicte ii,...Oddo, Mayole, Odilo, Hugo, Geralde, Leonarde, Guhtlace, Bernarde.

Virgins: Cirilla, Etheldreda, Mildburga, Radegundis, Walburgis, Florencia, Consortia, Daria, Columba.

428. Summa Raymundi   xiii   dari. m. v.

429. Legal. (1) Magna Charta etc.   xiv & xiii enim que ad
Initial of king. Partial border: so also in (3).
     (2) Ranulf de Glanville.   Placitum
     (3) Registrum Brevium.   caruc^i tenus

430. Gregorii Decretales   xiii   St Aug. Cant.
In a lovely hand: written in France. Wide margins and good pictured initials.   descendit ad
Title: Noue decretales cum C. D. XIIII. G. IIII. Liber S. Aug. Cant.
     Cat. f. 124.
     Ricardi Corne (?) ex dono Johannis Parker 29º Marcii 1596. TW. Johannes parker (in red chalk).
     At foot of f. 1 (xv): liber monasterii S. Aug. anglorum apostoli.
     Fly-leaves palimpsest over an old Kalendar (xi ?).
     On the leaf at end (October) are many obits e.g. XIIII. Kal. Nov. Theodorus Archiepiscopus.

431. Several volumes.
     (1) Aug.   xiv   sunt viciorum
     (2) Ailredi Speculum spiritualis
         amicitiae   xv
     (3) Prosper etc. Italian hand   xv   ? Ely
     Sum liber Joh. Stywarde militis ex dono dompni ducis Bedforde.
     Arms of Rob. Steward, last Prior of Ely.
     (4) Leo de conflictu viciorum, ff. 16   x, xi   Lanthony
     On last page: liber domus Lanthonie iuxta Glouc.   sem &
     Cat. no. 201.
     (5) Anselm etc.   xiii   in intimis

(6) Lucidaire in Latin and French xiii   ? Lanthony
Cf. Cat. p. 217, note 3.   M. Angelis
Many leaves at each end in various hands.

432. Paper, xv.

433. Constitutions. Original binding,   St Thomas of Acon ?
          skin over boards.   xv   altissimus
The last Constitution, added, is for the 'domus acon.'

434. Apocalypse, pictured   xiii
Iste liber est de communitate sororum Ev......P. 18.
Kershaw, p. 54 : contains 90 pictures, and closely resembles
MS. 177 at Eton College.

435. Psalter in Hebrew with Latin
          glosses   xiii
At the beginning are faintly pencilled names (xiii, xiv).
Galfridus fflayslond...Rad. del Wde....
Johannes   ...de horstede.
Rad. Wlkeder.
Rob. Dice de   to ldeshale (?) etc.
and contemporary notes on Hebrew vowels, etc.

436. Horologium Sapientiae.   Red
          skin over boards   xv   Witham
Liber cartusie de witham · orate pro Johanne Blacman.

                                                        eum s^i

437. (1) Aug. Meditations etc.   x   titudinem
    ' no. 535.'   Kershaw, p. 37.
       (2) Bernard de Considera-
                tione (1) etc.   xiii   nec deum timet
       (3) Bernard de Considera-
                tione (2). Round hand.
                Mut. init.   xiii
Marked Sancroft, fasc. 3. n. 10.

438. Processional   xv
A ' faburden ' at the end signed Willam Dundy.

439. Summa Gaufridi   xiii   ut c. de ue
    Rob. Hypkyn.   Precium istius libri x⁸ iiij^d.

440. Ivonis Chronicon   xii   St Servan
                                              gente
    At top of f. 1 (xiii): Liber S. Marie de S. Seruano ex dono
    Willelmi filii Dunecani quondam persone ipsius ecclesie.

441. Langton in xii Prophetas   xiv   ordine
    Table, and mark $ · xlvij in cover.

442. Chrysostom   xii   ? Lanthony
    In several hands.   Old table on fly-leaf.   pecuniam
    Lib. de....... ? Cat. no. 135.

443. Laurentius Dunelmensis   xii   quid deus
    On fly-leaf in pale ink (xiii): Quedam hystorie versificat'.
    Also: Danielis Rogerii A° 1563.

444. (1) Medica.   Paper and vellum   xv
      (2) *Cum mens artis*   xiii   ? Lanthony
    Marked '3 Bundle.'   2 fo. illegible

445-7. Paper, xvi, xvii.

448. Historia Eliensis etc.   Paper and
       vellum   xv, xvi   Ely
    Arms and epitaph of Robert Stewarde.

449. Decretum etc.   xiii   Lanthony
    In hoc. uol. continetur concordia discordancium canonum
etc.
    Also: M. de Kermerd, erased.

450. Laurentius de Savona.   Roman
       hand.   xv
    Waynflete's arms in initial: Letter to him of 1485.
    Alani Copei iste liber (xvi).

451. (1) Hieronymus contra Jovini-
         anum   xii   Lanthony
    Cat. no. 161.   recipimus
      (2) Bernard, etc.   xii   q'm et diuersa

452. Bernardus in Cantica   xii   Lanthony
      xvth cent. title.   At end (xv): Joh. Glowcet^r.   apud deum
      Cat. no. 140.

453. Paper, xvii.

454. (1) Almanack, English. W.
           Cant. (Laud or Sancroft),
           with elaborate volvels   xv
      (2) Galfridus Monumetensis   xiii   Eneas
      Bundle 2. 1.
      (3) Old title : *Historia Bruti*   xii   britannis
           prophecia merlini.

455. Horae. Coarse English work
           and pictures   xv
      ' Alene ' occurs in the Litany. Kershaw, p. 44.

456. (1) Priscian   xiii   heronius
      (2) Porphyry. Old title : Por-
           phirius   xiii   est quoddam
      (3) Dicta philosophorum. Pa-
           per. French   xv

457. (1) Paper.
      (2) Mauricii Sermones :   in
           French. Mut. init.   xiii
           ' Bundle 3.'
      (3) ' Seneca ad lucillum ' etc.
           Small hand   xiii early   tis nec
                                                        gratia

458. Summa Theologiae etc.   Large
           hand   xii, xiii   et infra

459. Horae. English. Pictures of the
           Passion in the text   xv
      Rather interesting.   Kershaw, p. 36.

460. Compilatio in Joh. Peckham   xv
      An ugly book.

461. Greek. Paper.

462. Paper, xvi.

463. Atlas. Fine title with Garter
and Arms of France and
England quarterly   xvi
Robert Hare 1564. Contains (1) Table, (2) 12 maps, (3)
compass in cover inscribed in English. No doubt by Baptista
Agnese.

464, 5. Paper, xvii.

466. Musica W. Chelle. Paper, xvi.

467–70. Paper, xvii.

471. (1) Virgil. Title (xiii) on f. 1
     at bottom   xii   Florentem
Picture of Meliboeus, and Tityrus piping.
     (2) Alexandreis   xii, xiii   Primus
         or Interior.

472. W. Hilton. Well written   xv
f. 260. This boke was maad of the goodis of Jon Killum,
etc.

At end a note that 'this boke be deliuered to Richard Colop
Parchemanere of London after my discesse.'

Also ' per me dom. Joh. Graunt. 1493.'

473. Summa de Vitiis. Mut. init.   xiii
At end a note of obits of John Rychemund, Rob. Keteryng,
monks 'monasterii appostolorum petri et pauli.' Also the
names Roger Byrde, Rich. Oxford.

474. Horae. Kershaw, p. 39.

475. (1) W. Hilton   xv
Joh. Barkham 1612.
     (2) Vita Roberti Bethune.
         Large hand   xii   Lanthony
Title: Vita domini Roberti de Bethune herfordensis Epi-
scopi.   gentia
Cf. Cat. no. 341.

476. Bible. Minute hand.   xiii   inter omnes

477. Pictor in Carmine (ff. 3–11)   xiii
      Themata,
      Concordance,
and much else, in small hands.

478. (1) Andreas Floccus   xv late
      Liber Will. Horman (Head Master of Eton).
      (2) Lyndwood's Provincial.

479. Lyndwood   xv late
      At end is ' Alma redemptoris mater,' with musical notes.

480. Sermons. (*Hora est*)   xiii   et erexit

481. Hugo de S. Victore etc. Many
          hands   xiii etc.   Lanthony
      xv^{th} cent. title on last page.
      LIBER NONUS at top, and old title in red.

482. Epistolae Pontificum   xv–xvi   Canterbury
      Foreign : good stamped binding with IHESUS MARIA.
      Matthaeus Davis.

483. Lincolniensis. Oculus Moralis,
          etc.   xiv   Durham
      Liber S. Cuthberti Dunelm. ...cuius usus conceditur
      domino Roberto Ebchester.   De coralium *or* duricia

484. Pore Caitif etc.   xv

485. Flores Bernardi. Small, like a
          Bible   xiii   ? Lanthony
      Cf. Cat. no. 141.   solus

486. Albertus in Sententias   xiii   ? Thurgarton
                                                    nomen tribuo
      Constat Ric. Forsett Canonicus (?) de Th......ton (xv).

487. Saxon Homilies. (*Cum appro-
          pinquasset*)   xii, xiii   on þisse liue

488. Sermons etc. Paper and vellum xiii   Buildwas
      The vellum sermons are ' monasterii de buldewas per d.

Joh. quowsal abbatem.' Given to Henr. de Valle, monachus
Sarresmace (?).

489. Saxon Homilies. A small book,
well written, inner corners of
the leaves mutilated xi

490. Paper, xvi, xvii.

491. Chron. etc. Paper and vellum xv

492. Hampole xv

493. Brute Chronicle xv late quod demones
John St Leger. Petrus Shee.

494–5. Paper xvi, xvii.

496. Horae. Foreign, not good xvi
Kershaw, p. 65.

497. Ailred etc. Sermons. Binding :
skin over boards xii, xiii Reading
hic est liber S. Marie de Rading. plagis

498. Paupertas xiv St Aug. Cant.
De librario S. Aug. Cant. dist. 9. g. 6. et pereuntibus
Cat. f. 57.

499. Collections. Bound in skin over
boards xii om. de uero
Old table on a label sewed to f. 1. Minute hand, much
contracted.

500. Hampole. Very neat xiv facti sumus

501. Secreta Secretorum. English xv
'Sheldonianus.' John Campe.

502. Grammatica. Many hands xii, xiii
Apparently a lot of fragments.

503. Galfridus Monumetensis xiv Shaftesbury
Liber d. Ricardi ap Robert Cantariat. s. anne infra monast.
Shaftonie. redes
Given by Fr. Bernard in 1684. W. Lambard 1566, Th.
Lambard 1637.

504. Robert de Aluesbury   xiv   Qe touz
On f. 1 (xvi): ·9· Rob. de Aluesbury.

505. Michael de Massa   1430   Sall (Norf.)
'Fecit fieri Mag. Will. de Wode, Rector de Salle, quem
scripsit Edmundus Southwelle in Rectoria de Salle. a. d. 1430.
In skin over boards : circuit edge.   Given by Sheldon.

506. Will. Worcester   xv

507-21. Paper, xvi, xvii.

522. Grosseteste. French poem   xiv   St Aug. Cant.
Di. XVI. Gra. IIII.   Tractatus domini Lincoln. et multa alia
in Gallico. Erasure follows.   a adam
Small pictures in text :
    1. Lincolniensis teaching a crowd.
    2. f. 49. Monk adoring Crucifix.
    3. f. 65. Monk adoring Virgin and Child.
    4. f. 73. St Francis (?) preaching.
Cat. f. 112a.

523. Lincolniensis Oculus Moralis   xiv   nus in ceterorum

524-6. Paper, xvii.

527. Chronicle. French   xiv   trogis

528. IV Evangelia (Codex Ephesinus)
    Graece   xii

529. Lyra etc.   xv   studiosos
Italian. Initial with bust of Francis or Lyra.

530. Aurora   xii, xiii   venire
Erasure of two lines at bottom of f. 1.

531. Aurora. Vellum wrapper : very
    like the last. Mut. init.   xii, xiii

532. Wycliffite, xv. N. T. etc.

533. Bible   xiii   ille reseruauit

534. Bible   xiii, xiv   Arklow
On the fly-leaf an undertaking of the Prior and Dominicans

of 'Arclowe' to keep the anniversary of Robert Dowdall .etc.
(xiv).   dit et

535. Psalter. Small foreign pictures
        of the Passion   xv   English
    Kalendar Dominican.   Litany has Edmund, Fremund,
Wenefreda.
    Kershaw, p. 68.

536. Musica Ecclesiastica   xv   ad deum
    Mag. hugo barker.
    Dom. Joh. Laythlay.

537. Paper, xvii.

538. Constitutions. Mut. init.   xv   tur si

539. Hildebrandi in Matthaeum Hom.
        xli–lxxxiiii   xii   seminat
    In a very curious hand.   Notes of xiv, xv.

540. Psalterium Ivonis   xii   Lanthony
    Label on fly-leaf : psalterium Iuonis (David ?).   domine quid
    After the first word or two the rest of each verse is
indicated by initials only.
    Cat. no. 61.

541. Wycliffite, xiv.

542. Aug. Regula etc.   Mut. init.   xiii   ? Lanthony
                                                      sed sicut

543. Statutes, xv.

544. Bible   xiii   ceptis

545. Horae of Lewkenor family   xiv
    Picture of the Rood of Bromholm.   Kershaw, p. 66.

546. Devotions. English   late xv

547. Wycliffite N. T.   xiv

548. Arabic.

549. Paper, xvii.

550. Hugonis etc. Sermones. (*Ibo*
     mihi ad montem mirre)   xii   in valle
    Many hands. The Regula S. Augustini occurs.

551. Wycliffe Questiones   xv
    Wrapped in a leaf of Aug. xi–xii.

552–5. Paper and vellum, xvi, xvii.

556. Statutes   xvi

557. Collectanea. Mut. init. 'Bundle
      3ʳᵈ'   xiii   ? Lanthony
    On f. 187 : ' Coll. super matth. secundum fr. W. de Ethel.'

558. Psalter etc. Kershaw, p. 58   xiii   Chr. Ch. Cant.
                                                 qui non
    Rough pictures. Full page : Annunciation, Nativity, Angel
and Shepherds, Adoration of Magi, Massacre of Innocents, Jesse
tree, ' Psalterium dompni Joh. Holyngborne.' (Monk of Christ
Church.)
    There are other full page pictures at the Nocturnes. At
f. 140 the hand changes to one of xiv, xvᵗʰ cent.
    In the Litany :
    Martyrs : Thoma ii, Aelphegi ii.
    Confessors : Augustine cum sociis, Odo, Dunstane ii, Ed-
munde...Wlgani...Cuthbert, Swithun, Fursey, Wilfrid, Paulinus,
Romanus, Wlstan, Richard, Hugo...Cuthlace, Columban.
    Virgins : Etheldreda, Mildreda, Eadburga, Ositha, Fredes-
wida.
    Then follow Cantica Monialia, Hymns, Office of the dead, etc.

559. Horae. (Devotions)   xiv ?

560. Horae. On binding : IACOB IL-
      LUMINATOR ME FECIT   xv
    English verse at end.

561. Horae   xv early

562. xvi.

563. Psalter. Kershaw, p. 76. Ban-
      croft's initials on the cover   xiii   St Neots

Kalendar. Obits of Abbots of Bec and Abps.
31 July. Neotus in blue.
7 Dec. Transl. S. Neoti in red.

Hymns for St Neot at end.

Fine initials : at *Dixit dominus* is the Creation of Eve.

564. Registrum Brevium   xiii, xiv
Pretty initial and ornaments.

565-6. Paper, xvi.

567. Registrum Brevium. Larger   xiv
Belonged to Cosin.

568. Paper, xvii.

569-76*b.* Oriental

CODICES CAREWANI.

596. French poem on the Conquest
of Ireland. Mut. at each end   xiii

598. Bray's Conquest of Ireland   xv

622. Giraldus Cambrensis   xv   manus et

633. Iohn Yonge   xv
At end :
Gracia nulla perit nisi gracia Blakmonachorum⎫
Est et semper erit litill thank in fine laborum ⎭
        per me R Robart Rawson.

CODICES TENISONIANI.

643, 4. Bulls.

693. Petronius, paper   xvi
    Daniel Roger. John Lawson.

742. Siege of Thebes. Lydgate   xv

752. Frontinus. Old cover   xiii   ceptis
Vegetius.
Title on 2ⁿᵈ cover in ink.

756.　Bible　　　　　　　　　　xiii
　　　Biblia m^{ri} harison.

759.　Sallust　　　　　　　　　　xv　　　　Italian
　　　Title on fly-leaf (xv) in English hand.　　cum moribus

761.　Vita S. Edwardi　　　　　　xiii　Westminster and
　　　　　　　　　　　　　　　　　　　　Gloucester
　　　Left by Islip Abbot of Westminster with Th. Seabroke
　　　Abbot of Gloucester.　The inscription to this effect is, I think,
　　　by Robert Hare.　　　　　　　　　　　　　　laurentio

853.　English Verse　　　　　　　xv
　　　Ed. Furnivall, E. E. T. S.　Religious Pieces.

877.　Hugo de claustro animae　　xiv
　　　Small foreign book.

CODICES MISCELLANEI.

1106.　(1)　Flores Historiarum　　xiv　　　latinos
　　　W. Darelli (Prebendary of Canterbury d. 1566).
　　　N. Brigam (d. 1559).
　　　Earl of Clarendon.
　　　　(2)　Chronicle　　　　　　xii　　Peterborough
　　　'per me Eliam de Trikyngham.'　　　　dclxxix

1152.　Bible　　　　　　　　　　xiii　　　litteras

1158.　Psalter.　Mut.　2 columns　xiv, xv
　　　Sarum Litanies at end.

1170, 71.　Chronological Rolls.

CODICES MANNERS-SUTTONIANI.

1208.　Armachanus　　　　　　　late xv　　alienando

1212.　Canterbury Privileges　　　xiii　　Canterbury
　　　Lumley.

1213.　Documents　　　　　　　xiv　　St Aug. Cant.
　　　　　　　　　　　　　　　　　　　yname

In isto libello multa et diuersa sunt compilata undecunque collecta prout patet in secundo folio proxime subsequenti.

Et est liber fratris Will¹ de Byholte cuius anime propicietur deus Amen.

It was 'assigned' by W. de Byholte to Petrus de Wroteham.

At end, partly cut off, is:

Will¹ de Byholte—Itinera Justiciariorum.

(Unnumbered)

Gospels of MacDurnan x Chr. Ch. Cant.

In Parkerian binding, and marked with Parker's red chalk.

2 fo. Eliud

On f. 3 b

+ MÆIELBRIÐVS · MAC

DVRNANI · ISTV̄ · TEXTV̄

PER TRIꝶVADRV̄ · D̄O

DIGNE · DOGMATIZAT

✠ AST · AETHELSTANVS

ANGLOSÆXꝶA · REX · ET

RECTOR · DORVERNENSI

METROPOLI · DAT · ꝑ · ÆVV̄

At the end of Matthew is an Anglo-Saxon charter of Abp Wulfstan, and a Latin donation of Canute in the Christ Church hand.

See Kershaw, p. 27.

Westwood. Miniatures and ornaments of Anglo-Saxon and Irish MSS.

Pal. Soc.

ADDITIONAL NOTE.

I will here venture to add a short note of such other Lanthony MSS. as have come under my notice. I shall be very glad to hear of additions to the list.

Catalogue (printed by H. Omont).

45-47. Libri moralium Gregorii in tribus voluminibus magnis.
Probably two volumes at Trinity College, Oxford (39, 40), given by Fr. Baber, Chancellor of Gloucester.

107. Clemens super Actus Apostolorum, liber mediocris.
British Museum, Royal MS. 2. D. v. Probably autograph.

113. Jeronimus super Ezechielem, magnum volumen.
Trin. Coll. Oxford 68. Given by Baber.

114. Jeronimus super Danielem, magnum volumen.
Trin. Coll. Oxford 69. 'Liber Lantoniensis ecclesie.' Given by Baber.

117. Jeronimus super Mattheum, magnum volumen.
Trin. Coll. Oxford 33. Given by Baber.

148. Liber Ysidori de differenciis, mediocre volumen.
Cambridge University Library, Dd. 10. 25. 'Liber lantonie.'

158. Paschasius de corpore Domini [et Lanfrancus contra Berengarium].
Trin. Coll. Oxford 51. Given by Baber.

168. Aug. de verbis Domini et de verbis apostoli, magnum volumen.
Queen's Coll. Oxford 309.

225. Exceptiones Roberti de Bracii, mediocris liber.
British Museum, Royal MS. 8. D. viii.

234. Decreta W(alteri) prioris in uno volumine cooperto viridi pelle.
Corpus Christi College, Oxford, 154, containing many Lanthony documents.

p. 220, note [3]. Libri de jure terre qui dicitur Gracton (*l.* Bracton). Sold at the Phillipps' sale 1896, lot 136 : of cent. xiii, xiv : contained Lanthony documents.

In addition to this I have encountered other books too late to be included in the fourteenth century catalogue. These are :

Trinity College, Oxford.

13. Hymns and Prayers : were owned by John Leche.
14. Nicolai de Munshulle opus grammaticum : belonged to John Leche.
16[A]. R. Hampole's Prick of Conscience : belonged to John Leche.
49. Chaucer's Canterbury Tales : belonged to John Leche.

Corpus Christi College, Oxford.

83. Polychronicon (xv) : ' olim abbatiae Lanthoniensis.'
192. Rationale Lanthoniense (xiv).

Both these books were given by Henry Parry to the College. It is probable that among his other gifts some at least are from Lanthony. They are :

32.	Bernardi meditationes etc.	xiii
33.	Sermones etc.	xiii
36.	Sermons etc. in French	xiv early
38.	Regula S. Augustini	xiii
	Vita S. Thomae	? = Cat. no. 273
42.	Mariale	xiv
	Barlaam et Josaphat etc.	
44.	Sarum Pica	xv
48.	Paterius etc.	xiii

52. P. Lombardi Sententiae xiii
55. Ricardi de Pophis Summa xiv
(belonged to John Dee)
59. Anticlaudianus etc. xiii
? Cat. 316 a Gloucestershire book
62. Grammatica latina versifice xiii
? Cat. 442
68. Constantinus de febribus xiii
? Cat. 460
72. Jo. Andreae Summa xv
78. Brute Chronicle in French xv
103. Anon. Universalia etc. xv
107. Will. Heddun super Aristo- xiv
telem de Anima
114. Aristotelis Physica etc. xiii
119. Kelwarby super Priscianum xiii
etc.
[122. Gospels xi. Irish]
139. Cassiodorus de anima etc. xii
? Cat. 211
157. Chronicles of Worcester, and xii
Marianus Scotus
Probably from Worcester: belonged to T. Straynsham
(monk) who gave it to W. T. Powycke, monk of Great Malvern,
in 1480.
159. Historia scholastica xiv
a Gloucestershire book
162. Pupilla oculi xiv
194. Aug. de quantitate animae etc. xii
? Cat. 180

I. INDEX OF PLACES TO WHICH MANUSCRIPTS CAN BE TRACED.

II. INDEX OF OWNERS AND SCRIBES OF THE MANUSCRIPTS.

For EU product safety concerns, contact us at Calle de José Abascal, 56–1°,
28003 Madrid, Spain or eugpsr@cambridge.org.

www.ingramcontent.com/pod-product-compliance
Ingram Content Group UK Ltd.
Pitfield, Milton Keynes, MK11 3LW, UK
UKHW012336130625
459647UK00009B/315